# Contents

Some words are shown in bold, **like this**. You can find out what they mean by looking in the glossary.

# What is a painting?

A painting is a picture made with paints.

Some paintings are thousands of years old.

# Start with Art

# Painting

Isabel Thomas

## www.raintreepublishers.co.uk

Visit our website to find out more information about Raintree books.

## To order:

☎ Phone 0845 6044371
🖷 Fax +44 (0) 1865 312263
🖳 Email myorders@raintreepublishers.co.uk

Customers from outside the UK please telephone +44 1865 312262

Raintree is an imprint of Capstone Global Library Limited, a company incorporated in England and Wales having its registered office at 7 Pilgrim Street, London, EC4V 6LB – Registered company number: 6695582

Edited by Dan Nunn, Rebecca Rissman, and Catherine Veitch
Designed by Richard Parker
Picture research by Mica Brancic and Hannah Taylor
Originated by Capstone Global Library
Printed and bound in China by South China Printing Company Ltd

ISBN 978 1 406 22408 5 (hardback)
15 14 13 12 11
10 9 8 7 6 5 4 3 2 1

ISBN 978 1 406 22415 3 (paperback)
16 15 14 13 12
10 9 8 7 6 5 4 3 2 1

**British Library Cataloguing in Publication Data**
Thomas, Isabel, 1980-
Painting. -- (Start with art)
750-dc22
A full catalogue record for this book is available from the British Library.

**Acknowledgements**
We would like to thank the following for permission to reproduce photographs: Alamy Images pp. 6 (© Hemis/ Chagall®/© ADAGP, Paris and DACS, London 2011), 7 (© Stock Italia), 14 (The Art Gallery Collection); © Capstone Publishers pp. 20, 21, 22, 23 – background, 23 – surface (Karon Dubke); Corbis pp. 4 (Free Agents Limited), 9, 13, 23 – Imagine (Christie's Images), 10 (The Gallery Collection), 16; Shutterstock pp. 5 (© Juriah Mosin), 8, 23 – silk (© Adam Gryko), 11 (Lauren Jade Goudie), 12 (© CYC), 23 – gallery (© Shamleen), 23 – mural (© Manuel Fernandes), 23 – palette (© Perkus), 23 – shades (© Dariusz Gudowicz); The Art Archive pp. 18 (São Paulo Art Museum Brazil/Dagli Orti), 19 (Minneapolis Institute of Fine Art/Superstock); The Bridgeman Art Library pp. 15 (Van der Heydt Museum, Wuppertal, Germany), 17 (Mellon Coll., Nat. Gallery of Art, Washington DC, USA).

Front cover photograph of Blue Fox, 1911 (oil on canvas) by Franz Marc (1880–1916) reproduced with permission of The Bridgeman Art Library (Van der Heydt Museum, Wuppertal, Germany). Back cover photograph of a girl painting reproduced with permission of Shutterstock (© Juriah Mosin). Back cover photograph of a paint palette reproduced with permission of Shutterstock (© Adam Gryko).

Every effort has been made to contact copyright holders of material reproduced in this book. Any omissions will be rectified in subsequent printings if notice is given to the publisher.

A person who makes paintings is called an artist.

You can be an artist, too!

# Where can I see paintings?

People like to look at paintings.

You can often see paintings in a
museum or **gallery**.

Paintings are all around you, too.
Look for paintings outdoors.

This **mural** is painted on a building
in Italy.

# What do people use to make paintings?

Artists mix paints on a **palette** to make different colours.

They dip brushes in the paint and then start painting.

People paint on paper, canvas, and other **surfaces**.

This Chinese picture is painted on **silk**.

# How do people make paintings?

Artists make paintings in different ways.

Most paintings have lines, shapes, and colours.

Dripping, flicking, and splattering paint makes an exciting picture.

Does this painting make you think about moving or staying still?

# What do people paint?

Some artists paint pictures of things that they see.

They paint people, animals, places, and objects.

Some artists paint made-up
things, too.

This artist **imagined** a picture and
used painting to show us her ideas.

Paintings can show us what
something looks like.

This artist copied the shapes
and colours of a real hare.

Paintings do not have to look real.
A fox is not really purple!

Why do you think the artist has
painted the fox purple?

# How can paintings show feelings?

Shapes and lines can make us feel different things.

Swirls of paint show us these stars in the night sky.

Artists use colours to show feelings, too.

Different **shades** of blue tell us this girl is feeling sad.

# What can paintings tell us?

Paintings can tell us how people lived in the past.

These little boys were painted 250 years ago. Do boys wear clothes like this today?

Paintings can tell us what life is like in other places.

This artist painted pictures of life on an island called Tahiti.

# Start to paint!

Look at the picture of the fox on page 15, and other paintings by Franz Marc.

1.  Collect pictures of your favourite animal or look at real animals.

2.  Plan your painting. Use a piece of chalk to draw the shapes that make up an animal.

3. Now paint your animal. You do not have to use its real colours.

4. You could choose colours that show if the animal is sad, happy, fierce, shy, or excited.

5. Decide whether to use a colour for the **background**.

6. Display your picture in an animal **gallery**!

# Glossary

**background** part of a picture that shows what is behind the thing being painted

**gallery** place where art is displayed for people to look at

**imagine** make things up in your head

**mural** painting on a building or wall

**palette** special board where an artist mixes paints

**shades** different kinds of one colour. Light red and dark red are different shades of red.

**silk** fine, soft material made by silkworms

**surface** something that an artist paints on, such as paper, canvas, silk, or wood

# Find out more

**Book**

*Action Art: Painting,* Isabel Thomas (Raintree, 2005)

**Websites**

See more paintings by Franz Marc on this website:
www.ibiblio.org/wm/paint/auth/marc/

On this website you can have a go at creating your own work of art in the style of Jackson Pollock: www.jacksonpollock.org

You can explore portrait paintings on this website:
www.museumnetworkuk.org/portraits/

# Index